DATE			

Chickens

by
Gail Saunders-Smith

Pebble Books

an imprint of Capstone Press

Pebble Books are published by Capstone Press
151 Good Counsel Drive, P.O. Box 669, Mankato, Minnesota 56002
http://www.capstone-press.com

2 3 4 5 6 07 06 05 04 03 02

Library of Congress Cataloging-in-Publication Data
Saunders-Smith, Gail.
　　Chickens/by Gail Saunders-Smith.
　　p. cm.
　　Includes bibliographical references (p. 23) and index.
　　Summary: Describes the life cycle of the chicken through photographs and text.
　　ISBN 1-56065-483-X (hardcover)
　　ISBN 1-56065-954-8 (paperback)
　　1. Chickens—Juvenile literature. 2. Chickens—Life cycles—Juvenile literature.
[1. Chickens.] I. Title.
SF487 .5.S38 1997
636.5—dc21
　　　　　　　　　　　　　　　　　　　　　　　　　　97-8309
　　　　　　　　　　　　　　　　　　　　　　　　　　CIP
　　　　　　　　　　　　　　　　　　　　　　　　　　AC

Editorial Credits
Lois Wallentine, editor; Timothy Halldin and James Franklin, designers;
Michelle L. Norstad, photo researcher

Photo Credits
George White Location Photography, 1, 6
Dwight Kuhn, 10, 12
Unicorn Stock/Martha McBride, 4, 8
Valan Photos/Jim Fowler, cover, 18; Michael J. Johnson, 14, 16; Wouterloot-Gregoire, 20

Table of Contents

Roosters crow.

Hens cluck.

Hens sit.

Chicks peck.

Chicks hatch.

Chicks grow.

16

Chicks drink and grow.

Chicks eat and grow.

Roosters crow. Hens cluck.

Words to Know

chick—a young chicken

chicken—a kind of bird that is raised on farms

cluck—a sound a hen makes

crow—a sound a rooster makes

egg—the first stage of a chicken

hatch—to come out of an egg

hen—a female chicken

peck—when a chicken strikes or picks something up with its beak

rooster—a male chicken

Read More

Hariton, Anca. *Egg Story.* New York: Dutton Children's Books, 1992.

Legg, Gerald. *From Egg to Chicken.* Lifecycles. New York: Franklin Watts, 1998.

Wood, A.J. *Egg!* Boston: Little Brown and Company, 1993.

Internet Sites

American Egg Board
http://www.aeb.org/

Poultry Page
http://www.cyborganic.net/people/feathersite/
Poultry/BRKPoultryPage.html

Note to Parents and Teachers

This book describes and illustrates the life cycle of a chicken with photographs and text. The clear photographs support the beginning reader in making and maintaining the meaning of the text. The plural noun and simple verb directly match the photograph on each page. Children may need assistance in using the Table of Contents, Words to Know, Read More, Internet Sites, and Index/Word List sections of the book.

Index/Word List

Word Count: 24
Early-Intervention Level: 6